Descendants of Edward William Savage

Generation 1

1. **EDWARD WILLIAM[1] SAVAGE** was born on 22 Nov 1843 in Cadaretta, Choctaw County, Mississippi.
    He died on 21 Aug 1915 in Whitewright, Fannin County, Texas. He married Martha Jane
    Trussell, daughter of Henry H. Trussell and Jane Stanley Smith on 27 Feb 1866 in Yalobusha
    County, Mississippi. She was born on 30 Dec 1841 in Graysport, Mississippi. She died on 16
    Jan 1925 in Whitewright, Texas.

    More About Edward William Savage:
    Burial: 22 Aug 1915 in Oak Hill Cemetery, Whitewright, Fannin County, Texas
    Occupation: 1860 in Township 21, Choctaw County, Mississippi; Farm Worker
    Occupation: 1870 in Township 21, Range 8, Choctaw County, Mississippi;
    Farmer
    Occupation: 1880 in Precinct 5, Grayson County, Texas; Farmer
    Occupation: 1900 in Justice Precinct 3, Grayson County, Texas; Farmer
    Occupation: 1910 in Justice Precinct 3, Grayson County, Texas; Farmer
    Military Service: Bet. 18 Aug 1861-16 Jun 1865; Sergeant, Company K, 15th Mississippi
    Inf. C.S.A.
    Property: 1875 in Grayson County, Texas; 80 Acres
    Property: 1876 in Grayson County, Texas; 80 Acres
    Property: 1877 in Grayson County, Texas; 80 1/3 Acres
    Property: 1880 in Grayson County, Texas; 65 Acres Improved and 10 Acres Unimproved

    Notes for Edward William Savage: Moved
    to Grayson County, Texas in 1872.

    Enlisted in Company K, 15th Mississippi Infantry August 18, 1861 in Corinth,
    Mississippi. Wounded at Mill Springs, Tennessee.
    Wounded in right leg on November 30, 1864 and captured at Franklin, Tennessee on
    December 17, 1864. Held prisoner in Nashville, Tennessee until May 6, 1865 when he was
    transferred to Louisville, Kentucky
    Developed Smallpox in January 1865 while a prisoner of war in Nashville, Tennessee.
    Released from prisoner of war status at Louisville, Kentucky on June 16, 1865.

    1843 is the correct birth year for Edward William Savage. He used 1840 as a birth year because
    he was younger than his wife and got tired of hearing about it. Family headstone has 1840 as
    year of birth. Military headstone has 1843 as year of birt

    More About Martha Jane Trussell:
    Burial: 17 Jan 1925 in Oak Hill Cemetery, Whitewright, Fannin County, Texas

    Notes for Martha Jane Trussell:
    Headstone has December 30, 1840 as date of birth. Death certificate has December 30, 1841
    as date of birth.

    Edward William Savage and Martha Jane Trussell had the following children:

2.   i. CHARLES EDWARD[2] SAVAGE was born on 10 Jan 1867 in Grenada, Mississippi. He died on
    01 Mar 1919 in Sherman, Texas. He married Flora Belle Payne, daughter of William
    Payne and Mary Francis Weatherly on 15 Feb 1893 in Grayson County, Texas. She
    was born on 15 Dec 1868 in Lone Oak, Texas. She died on 30 Dec 1938 in Sherman,
    Texas.

3.   ii. ROBERT CIDNEY SAVAGE was born on 21 May 1868 in Grenada, Mississippi. He died on
    24 Apr 1950 in Riverside County, California. He married (1) MOLLY CRAIG,

daughter of John Craig on 26 Sep 1888 in Sherman, Texas. She was born in Nov 1869 in Texas. He married (2) MAY HARPER on 17 Aug 1907 in Atoka County, Oklahoma. She was born about 1868 in Texas. She died before 06 Jan 1920.

4.   iii. MARY VIRGINIA SAVAGE was born on 20 Oct 1869 in Grenada, Mississippi. She died on 13 May 1931 in Sherman, Texas. She married (1) FRANK C. SHORT, son of William Short and Mahaly Elizabeth Williams about 1901 in Grayson County, Texas. He was born on 23 Apr 1866 in Murfreesboro, Rutherford County, Tennessee. He died on 06 Oct 1936 in Sherman, Texas. She married (2) CHARLES E. MATHIS on 05 Sep 1886 in Grayson County, Texas. He was born on 04 Mar 1863 in Mississippi. He died on 08 Jun 1898 in Fannin County, Texas.

5.   iv. NORA LEA SAVAGE was born on 21 Jul 1871 in Mississippi. She died on 28 Aug 1933 in Knox City, Knox County, Texas. She married William Hicks Bray, son of James Bray and Mary Wilson on 06 Nov 1890 in Grayson County, Texas. He was born on 08 Jan 1868 in Texas. He died on 14 May 1941 in Lubbock, Texas.

6.   v. JOHN HENRY SAVAGE was born on 23 Feb 1873 in Whitewright, Texas. He died on 26 Aug 1941 in Denison, Grayson County, Texas. He married Hattie Jim Marshall, daughter of Crockett Marshall and (unknown) on 29 Mar 1896 in Grayson County, Texas. She was born on 15 Dec 1872 in Greensboro, Kentucky. She died on 24 Nov 1962 in Denison, Grayson County, Texas.

       vi. BENJAMIN FRANKLIN SAVAGE was born on 07 Dec 1874 in Whitewright, Texas. He died on 26 Dec 1935 in Whitewright, Texas. He married Bertha Caylor, daughter of William W. Caylor and Martha C. Howard in Aft. June 19, 1920 and Bef. April 23, 1930. She was born on 25 Oct 1889 in North Carolina. She died on 01 Sep 1953 in Whitewright, Texas.

More About Benjamin Franklin Savage:
Burial: 27 Dec 1935 in Oak Hill Cemetery, Whitewright, Fannin County, Texas Cause Of Death: Nephritis
Occupation: 1900 in Sherman, Grayson County, Texas; Lawyer
Occupation: 1910 in Dallas, Dallas County, Texas; Lawyer
Occupation: 1918 in Whitewright, Grayson County, Texas; Attorney
Occupation: 1930 in San Angelo, Tom Green County, Texas; Attorney

Notes for Benjamin Franklin Savage:
World War One draft registration has birth date of December 1, 1874. 1900 U.S. census has a birth date of December 1874. Headstone has a birth date of December 7, 1873. Death certificate has birth date of December 7, 1873.

7.   vii. EDWARD SAVAGE was born on 26 Oct 1876 in Whitewright, Texas. He died on 08 Jan 1936 in Dallas, Texas. He married Mabel Seretha DeHaven, daughter of Charles DeHaven and Mary Elizabeth Clark on 14 Jul 1895 in Grayson County, Texas. She was born on 21 Jun 1878 in Denison, Texas. She died on 09 Nov 1944 in Dallas, Texas.

Generation 2

2.   CHARLES EDWARD[2] SAVAGE (Edward William[1]) was born on 10 Jan 1867 in Grenada, Mississippi. He died on 01 Mar 1919 in Sherman, Texas. He married Flora Belle Payne, daughter of William Payne and Mary Francis Weatherly on 15 Feb 1893 in Grayson County, Texas. She was born on

15 Dec 1868 in Lone Oak, Texas. She died on 30 Dec 1938 in Sherman, Texas.

More About Charles Edward Savage:
Burial: 03 Mar 1919 in West Hill Cemetery, Sherman, Grayson County,
Texas Cause Of Death: Heart Attack
Occupation: 1880; Farm Worker, Grayson County, Texas
Occupation: 1900 in Whitewright, Grayson County, Texas; Hardware
Salesman
Occupation: 1905 in Sherman, Grayson County, Texas; Salesman
Occupation: 1910 in Sherman, Grayson County, Texas; Hardware Salesman at Hardwicke
and Etter Hardware Company
Occupation: 1912 in Sherman, Grayson County, Texas; Clerk at Hardwicke and Etter
Hardware Company
Occupation: 1914 in Sherman, Grayson County, Texas; Bookkeeper for Hardwicke and
Etter Hardware Company
Occupation: 1916 in Sherman, Grayson County, Texas; Clerk at Hardwicke and Etter
Hardware Company
Occupation: 1916 in Sherman, Grayson County, Texas; Councilman
Occupation: 1918 in Sherman, Grayson County, Texas; City Clerk

More About Flora Belle Payne:
Burial: 31 Dec 1938 in West Hill Cemetery, Grayson County,
Texas
Cause Of Death: Coronary Occlusion
Living In: 1920 Living with her minor children, Nina Lea and William, as a widow in Sherman,
Grayson County, Texas
Living In: 1930 Living with her daughter, Nina Lea, and her husband in Okemah, Okfuskee
County, Oklahoma

Notes for Flora Belle Payne:
Living with Al Bryan and family in Okemah, Oklahoma in 1930.

Charles Edward Savage and Flora Belle Payne had the following children:

8.   i. MAUDE ALEENE[3] SAVAGE was born on 27 Jul 1894 in Whitewright, Texas. She died on 29
           Jan 1977 in Sherman, Texas. She married (1) JOSEPH BLEDSOE THORN, son of David
           Dancy Thorn and Ida Susan Bledsoe on 18 May 1916 in Sherman, Texas. He was
           born on 30 Dec 1892 in Eureka Springs, Arkansas. He died on 13 Nov 1976 in
           Whitesboro, Grayson County, Texas. She married (2) CHARLES BATSELL WINSTEAD,
           son of Washington Lee Winstead and May Merle Tutt on 09 Aug 1970. He was born
           on 25 May 1891 in Sherman, Texas. He died on 03 Aug 1973 in Albuquerque, New
           Mexico.

9.   ii. FLORA CLYDE SAVAGE was born on 26 Feb 1896 in Whitewright, Texas. She died on 15
           Jan 1987 in Dallas, Texas. She married Claude Augustus Brewer, son of William Eller
           Brewer and Maude Elizabeth Carson on 13 Jan 1918 in Sherman, Texas. He was born
           on 24 Sep 1895 in Cumby, Hopkins County, Texas. He died on 30 Dec 1969 in Dallas,
           Texas.

10.   iii. NINA LEA SAVAGE was born on 07 May 1900 in Whitewright, Texas. She died on 02 Jul
           1982 in Edmond, Oklahoma. She married Al Bryan on 06 Nov 1921 in Sherman,
           Texas. He was born on 23 Jan 1899 in Texas. He died on 07 Dec 1982 in Edmond,
           Oklahoma.

11.   iv. WILLIAM PAYNE SAVAGE was born on 23 Sep 1903 in Whitewright, Texas. He died in Jul
           1970 in Oklahoma City, Oklahoma. He married Mary Bell Badgett, daughter of Claude
           Ray Badgett and Annie Bell Bowie on 28 Feb 1925 in Bells, Grayson

County, Texas. She was born on 19 Oct 1905 in Bells, Texas. She died on 20
Feb 1964 in Houston, Texas.

3. **ROBERT CIDNEY**[2] **SAVAGE** (Edward William[1]) was born on 21 May 1868 in Grenada, Mississippi.
    He died on 24 Apr 1950 in Riverside County, California. He married (1) **MOLLY CRAIG**, daughter of
    John Craig on 26 Sep 1888 in Sherman, Texas. She was born in Nov 1869 in Texas. He married
    (2) **MAY HARPER** on 17 Aug 1907 in Atoka County, Oklahoma. She was born about 1868 in
    Texas. She died before 06 Jan 1920.

    More About Robert Cidney Savage:
    Living In: 1940 Living with his daughter, Nellie, and her husband in Palo Verde, Riverside
    County, California.
    Occupation: 1900 in Township 3, Choctaw Nation, Indian Territory (present day
    Oklahoma); Farmer
    Occupation: 1910 in Caney, Atoka County, Oklahoma; Printing Office Employee
    Occupation: 1920 in Caney, Atoka County, Oklahoma; General Laborer

    Robert Cidney Savage and Molly Craig had the following children:

    i.   LILLY[3] SAVAGE was born in Aug 1890 in Texas.

    ii.   RALPH VOLNEY SAVAGE was born on 22 Nov 1891 in Whitewright, Texas. He died
            on 24 Jul 1958 in Los Angeles County, California. He married FLORA ETHEL
            (UNKNOWN). She was born on 12 Jan 1895 in Missouri. She died on 12 Jun 1976
            in Los Angeles County, California.

            More About Ralph Volney Savage:
            Occupation: 1917 in Sedalia, Pettit County, Missouri; Automobile Mechanic

    iii.   NELLIE M. SAVAGE was born on 17 Dec 1899 in Indian Territory (present day
            Oklahoma). She died on 21 Sep 1963 in San Diego County, California. She
            married Victor C. Collier on 02 Feb 1919 in Sedalia, Pettis County, Missouri. He
            was born on 11 Mar 1888 in Alabama. He died on 16 Mar 1961 in San Diego
            County, California.

            More About Nellie M. Savage:
            Burial: Eternal Hills Memorial Park, Oceanside, San Diego County, California

4. **MARY VIRGINIA**[2] **SAVAGE** (Edward William[1]) was born on 20 Oct 1869 in Grenada, Mississippi. She
    died on 13 May 1931 in Sherman, Texas. She married (1) **FRANK C. SHORT**, son of William Short and
    Mahaly Elizabeth Williams about 1901 in Grayson County, Texas. He was born on 23 Apr 1866 in
    Murfreesboro, Rutherford County, Tennessee. He died on 06 Oct 1936 in Sherman, Texas. She
    married (2) **CHARLES E. MATHIS** on 05 Sep 1886 in Grayson County, Texas. He was born on
    4 Mar 1863 in Mississippi. He died on 08 Jun 1898 in Fannin County, Texas.

    More About Mary Virginia Savage:
    Burial: 14 May 1931 in West Hill Cemetery, Sherman,
    Texas Cause Of Death: Cancer of Uterus
    Living In: 1900 Mary and her children are living with her parents in Justice Precinct 3, Grayson
    County, Texas

    Notes for Mary Virginia Savage:

Living with parents in 1900.

More About Frank C. Short:
Burial: 07 Oct 1936 in West Hill Cemetery, Sherman, Texas
Occupation: 1900 in Justice Precinct 3, Grayson County Texas; Farmer
Occupation: 1910 in Justice Precinct 1, Grayson County, Texas; Farmer
Occupation: 1920 in Justice Precinct 1, Grayson County, Texas; Farmer
Occupation: 1921 in Sherman, Grayson County, Texas; Farmer
Occupation: 1925 in Sherman, Grayson County, Texas; Driver for Coca Cola Bottling
company
Occupation: 1926 in Sherman, Grayson County, Texas; Farmer
Occupation: 1930 in Sherman, Grayson County, Texas; Deputy
Sheriff.
Occupation: County Commissioner, Grayson County, Texas

More About Frank C. Short and Mary Virginia Savage:
m: 05 Sep 1886 in Grayson County, Texas

Frank C. Short and Mary Virginia Savage had the following children:

    i.   MARY[3] SHORT was born about 1902 in Texas.

        More About Mary Short:
        Occupation: 1920 in Justice Precinct 1, Grayson County, Texas; Office Girl
        in Lawyer's Office

    ii.   FRANK C. SHORT was born about 1906 in Texas.

More About Charles E. Mathis:
Burial: Oak Hill Cemetary, Whitewright, Texas

Charles E. Mathis and Mary Virginia Savage had the following children:

    i.   EDNA[3] MATHIS was born in Jul 1887 in Texas.

    ii.   JOHN LESTER MATHIS was born on 24 May 1889 in Whitewright, Texas. He died
        on 18 Aug 1946 in McKinney, Collin County, Texas.

        More About John Lester Mathis:
        Burial: 19 Aug 1946 in McKinney, Texas
        Living In: 1910 Living with his maternal grandparents in Justice Precinct 3,
        Grayson County, Texas.
        Occupation: 1900; Farm Laborer, Grayson County, Texas
        Occupation: 1917 in Sherman, Grayson County, Texas; Working for Prarie
        Auto Company

        Notes for John Lester Mathis:
        World War One draft registration has his name as John Lester Matthews but
        is signed John L. Mathis.

12.   iii. MARTHA MATHIS was born on 18 Jan 1893 in Whitewright, Texas. She died on 22 Sep
        1938 in Pahokee, Palm Beach County, Florida. She married CHARLES DENTON. He
        was born on 14 Jan 1895 in Tennessee. He died in Jan 1967 in Palm Beach County,
        Florida. She married (2) LUSTER RAY KERR in 1909. He was born on 21 Jul 1889 in
        Grayson County, Texas. He died on 23 Nov 1924 in San Angelo, Tom Green County,
        Texas.

5.   **NORA LEA**[2] **SAVAGE** (Edward William[1]) was born on 21 Jul 1871 in Mississippi. She died on 28 Aug 1933 in Knox City, Knox County, Texas. She married William Hicks Bray, son of James Bray and Mary Wilson on 06 Nov 1890 in Grayson County, Texas. He was born on 08 Jan 1868 in Texas. He died on 14 May 1941 in Lubbock, Texas.

More About Nora Lea Savage:
Burial: 29 Aug 1933 in Johnson Memorial Cemetery, Munday, Knox County,
Texas Cause Of Death: General Peritonitis from Ruptured Appendix

Notes for Nora Lea Savage:
Family has her name as Nora Lea. Head stone and death certificate have her name as Nora Lee.

More About William Hicks Bray:
Burial: 15 May 1941 in Johnson Memorial Cemetery, Munday, Knox County,
Texas
Cause Of Death: Cerebral Hemorrhage
Occupation: 1880 in Grayson County, Texas; Works on Farm
Occupation: 1900 in Justice Precinct 6, Grayson County, Texas; Farmer
Occupation:1910 in Chillicothe Ward 3, Hardeman County, Texas; Retail Grocery
Salesman
Occupation: 1920 in Munday, Knox County, Texas; Grocery Store Salesman
Occupation: 1930 in Munday, Knox County, Texas; Merchantile
Collector
Occupation: 1940 in Bowie, Montague County, Texas; Retired

William Hicks Bray and Nora Lea Savage had the following children:

    i.   CORDAS LESTER[3] BRAY was born on 19 Oct 1894 in Whitewright, Texas. He died on 05 Oct 1960 in Kern County, California.

        More About Cordas Lester Bray:
        Burial: Greenlawn Memorial Park, Bakersfield, Kern County, California

    ii.   BIRDIE F. BRAY was born on 02 Jun 1892 in Texas. She died on 10 Sep 1976 in Kern County, California. She married THOMAS HENDRIX LOCKARD. He was born on 12 Nov 1885 in Missouri. He died on 04 May 1936 in Tolbert, Wilbarger County, Texas.

        More About Birdie F. Bray:
        Burial: Greenlawn Memorial Park, Bakersfield, Kern County, California

    iii.   GETA BRAY was born on 16 Jul 1896 in Texas. She died on 02 Aug 1985 in Texas. She married FRED NOBLE WARREN. He was born on 13 Apr 1891. He died on 20 Jun 1986 in Texas.

        More About Geta Bray:
        Burial: Lakewood Memorial Park, Henderson, Rusk County, Texas

6.   **JOHN HENRY**[2] **SAVAGE** (Edward William[1]) was born on 23 Feb 1873 in Whitewright, Texas. He died on 26 Aug 1941 in Denison, Grayson County, Texas. He married Hattie Jim Marshall, daughter of Crockett Marshall and (unknown) on 29 Mar 1896 in Grayson County, Texas. She was born on 15 Dec 1872 in Greensboro, Kentucky. She died on 24 Nov 1962 in Denison, Grayson County, Texas.

More About John Henry Savage:

Burial: 27 Aug 1941 in Oak Hill Cemetery, Whitewright, Fannin County,
Texas Cause Of Death: Cancer of Face
Occupation: 1900 in Justice Precinct 3, Grayson County, Texas; Farmer
Occupation: 1910 in Justice Precinct 3, Grayson County, Texas; Farmer
Occupation: 1920 in Justice Precinct 3, Grayson County, Texas; Farmer
Occupation: 1930 in Denison, Grayson County, Texas; Road Laborer
Occupation: 1940 in Denison, Grayson County, Texas; Laborer in City Park

More About Hattie Jim Marshall:
Burial: 25 Nov 1962 in Oak Hill Cemetery, Whitewright, Fannin County,
Texas Cause Of Death: Congestive Heart Failure

John Henry Savage and Hattie Jim Marshall had the following children:

      i. LINTON LEE[3] SAVAGE was born on 07 Nov 1896 in Whitewright, Texas. He died on 25 Mar 1967 in Sherman, Texas. He married Lenora Kinghorn, daughter of John Scott Kinghorn and Emma M. Valentine on 08 Feb 1919 in Sherman, Texas. She was born on 31 Aug 1896 in Albany, Indian territory (Oklahoma). She died on 27 Mar 1973 in Grayson County, Texas.

      More About Linton Lee Savage:
      Burial: 27 Mar 1967 in West Hill Cemetery, Sherman, Texas
      Cause Of Death: Myocardial Infarction
      Occupation: Car Salesman
      Military Service: World War One

      ii. MARY BELLE SAVAGE was born on 17 Dec 1899. She married HENRY BOWMAN.

      iii. EDWIN LUTHER SAVAGE was born on 29 Dec 1909 in Whitewright, Texas. He died on 30 Jul 1979 in Denison, Grayson County, Texas. He married ALENE GRACE GILSTRAP. She was born on 21 Jul 1906 in Royse City, Texas. She died on 09 Aug 1976 in Denison, Grayson County, Texas.

      More About Edwin Luther Savage:
      Burial: 03 Aug 1979 in Oakwood Cemetery, Denison, Grayson County, Texas
      Occupation: ; Truck Driver

7.   EDWARD[2] SAVAGE (Edward William[1]) was born on 26 Oct 1876 in Whitewright, Texas. He died on 08 Jan 1936 in Dallas, Texas. He married Mabel Seretha DeHaven, daughter of Charles DeHaven and Mary Elizabeth Clark on 14 Jul 1895 in Grayson County, Texas. She was born on 21 Jun 1878 in Denison, Texas. She died on 09 Nov 1944 in Dallas, Texas.

More About Edward Savage:
Burial: 09 Jan 1936 in Oak Hill Cemetery, Whitewright, Fannin County,
Texas
Cause Of Death: Bronchial Pneumonia and Nephritis
Occupation: 1900 in Justice Precinct 3, Grayson County, Texas; Farmer
Occupation: 1910 in Whitewright, Grayson County, Texas; House Painter
Occupation: 1920 in Denison, Grayson County, Texas; Painter and Paper Hanging
Contractor
Occupation: 1930 in Precinct 2, Grayson County, Texas; Farmer
Occupation: Building Contractor

Notes for Edward Savage:
Sometimes known as Edwin or Ed Savage. World War One draft registration has first name as

Edward. Headstone and death certificate have first name as Ed.

More About Mabel Seretha DeHaven:
Burial: 11 Nov 1944 in Oak Hill Cemetery, Whitewright, Fannin County,
Texas Cause Of Death: Uremia after Removal of Gall Bladder.
Living In: 1940 Living as a widow in Dallas, Dallas County, Texas

Notes for Mabel Seretha DeHaven:
Her death Certificate and her husband's World War One draft registration spell her first name as Mabel. Headstone spells her first name as Mable. Death certificate of her son, Lester, spells her first name as Mabel. Death cerrtificates of her son, Herbert, and her daughter, Lorene, spell her first name as Mable.

Edward Savage and Mabel Seretha DeHaven had the following children:

13.   i. IRENE FAE[3] SAVAGE was born on 10 Dec 1896 in Whitewright, Texas. She died on 24 Oct 1976 in Westville, Oklahoma. She married Henry Lightfoot Large, son of Jonathan A. Large and Sophrona Elizabeth Gossett on 03 Oct 1920 in Texas. He was born on 26 Jun 1895 in Mulberry, Fannin County, Texas. He died on 14 Mar 1963 in Westville, Oklahoma.

      ii. CLEATUS SAVAGE was born in Jan 1899 in Texas.

14.   iii. HERBERT BURTIS SAVAGE was born on 24 Aug 1900 in Texas. He died on 16 Oct 1960 in Grand Prarie, Dallas County, Texas. He married BESSIE LOU HICKS. She was born on 31 Jan 1901 in Tom Bean, Texas. She died on 05 Feb 1959 in Dallas, Dallas County, Texas.

15.   iv. VELMA SAVAGE was born on 25 Jan 1902 in Bells, Grayson County, Texas. She died on 18 Apr 1983 in Mesa, Arizona. She married James Thomas Watson, son of Morton Price Watson and Amanda Allethia Goff on 07 Sep 1919 in Denison, Texas. He was born on 11 Oct 1896 in Bells, Grayson County, Texas. He died on 17 Aug 1973 in Mesa, Arizona.

      v. LORENE MARIE SAVAGE was born on 14 Aug 1909 in Texas. She died on 20 Jan 1961 in Dallas, Dallas County, Texas. She married JAMES F. NEWBERRY. He was born about 1907 in Texas.

More About Lorene Marie Savage:
Burial: 23 Jan 1961 in Restland Memorial Park, Dallas, Dallas County, Texas
Living In: 1961 Irving, Texas
Occupation: 1961; Secretary at Retail Merchant Association

      vi. OLLIE MAE SAVAGE was born on 02 Oct 1913 in Texas. She died on 05 Mar 2000 in Dallas County, Texas. She married James Eugene Poteet on 09 Mar 1944 in Dallas County, Texas. He was born on 08 Apr 1916 in Falls City, Nebraska. He died on 11 Mar 2001 in Texas.

More About Ollie Mae Savage:
Burial: Restland Memorial Park, Dallas, Dallas County, Texas
Living In: 1940 Living with her mother in Dallas, Dallas County, Texas
Occupation: 1940 in Dallas, Dallas County. Texas; Stenographer at Wholesale and Retail Machinery Company

16.   vii. LESTER EDWARD SAVAGE was born on 04 May 1916 in Texas. He died on 22 Sep 1981 in Dallas, Dallas County, Texas. He married FRANCES LOUISE DEARING. She died after 22 Sep 1981.

         viii. GEORGIA LEE SAVAGE was born on 09 Nov 1917 in Denison, Grayson County, Texas. She died on 01 May 1992 in Dallas County, Texas. She married (UNKNOWN) SLEDGE.

         ix. LURA EUGENE SAVAGE was born about Nov 1919 in Texas.

         More About Lura Eugene Savage:
Living In: 1940 Living with her mother in Dallas, Dallas County, Texas
Occupation: 1940 in Dallas, Dallas County, Texas; Nurse in Hospital Work and Private Practice

Generation 3

8.   MAUDE ALEENE[3] SAVAGE (Charles Edward[2], Edward William[1]) was born on 27 Jul 1894 in Whitewright, Texas. She died on 29 Jan 1977 in Sherman, Texas. She married (1) JOSEPH BLEDSOE THORN, son of David Dancy Thorn and Ida Susan Bledsoe on 18 May 1916 in Sherman, Texas. He was born on 30 Dec 1892 in Eureka Springs, Arkansas. He died on 13 Nov 1976 in Whitesboro, Grayson County, Texas. She married (2) CHARLES BATSELL WINSTEAD, son of Washington Lee Winstead and May Merle Tutt on 09 Aug 1970. He was born on 25 May 1891 in Sherman, Texas. He died on 03 Aug 1973 in Albuquerque, New Mexico.

More About Maude Aleene Savage:
Burial: 01 Feb 1977 in West Hill Cemetery, Grayson County, Texas
Occupation: 1940 in Sherman, Grayson County, Texas; Recreation Leader on Recreation Project

More About Joseph Bledsoe Thorn:
Burial: 15 Nov 1976 in Oakwood Cemetery, Whitesboro, Grayson County, Texas
Living In: 1940 Living with his mother in Grayson County, Texas
Occupation: 1920 in Justice Precinct 7, Grayson County, Texas; Farmer
Occupation: 1930 in Precinct 7, Grayson County, Texas; Farmer
Occupation: 1940 in Justice Precinct 7, Grayson County, Texas; Cotton Converter

Joseph Bledsoe Thorn and Maude Aleene Savage had the following children:

17.   i. JOSEPH WILLIAM[4] THORN was born on 09 May 1917 in Sherman, Grayson County, Texas. He died on 29 Oct 1952 in Fort Worth, Tarrant County, Texas. He married Edith Jewell Dick on 10 Sep 1937 in Thackerville, Oklahoma. She was born on 19 Oct 1920 in Denison, Texas.

18.   ii. ALBERT BLEDSOE THORN was born on 30 Nov 1918 in Dexter, Grayson County, Texas. He died on 27 Jul 2009 in Garland, Texas. He married (1) HANNELORE HEDWIG MAHLOW on 29 Mar 1950. She was born on 11 Nov 1923 in Germany. He married (2) CAROLYN S. MCADAMS on 20 Sep 1981 in Dallas County, Texas. She was born on 17 Oct 1944.

19.   iii. PATRICIA ALTON THORN was born on 16 Oct 1923 in Dexter, Grayson County, Texas. She died on 18 Aug 2013 in Athens, Henderson County, Texas. She married Kenneth Leroy Jones, son of Howard Lyman Jones and Rebecca Glen Herron on 13 Apr 1946 in Dade County, Florida. He was born on 29 Jul 1920 in Long Branch, New Jersey. He died on 03 Mar 1998 in Sherman, Texas.

20.   iv. THOMAS PAYNE THORN was born on 30 Dec 1925 in Delaware Bend, Texas. He died on 28 Sep 1990 in Galveston, Texas. He married NANCY COQUESE MCLANE. She was born on 13 Mar 1926 in Sherman, Texas. She died on 15 Jan 1979 in Harbor City, Los Angeles County, California. He married SANDRA WALSH.

More About Charles Batsell Winstead:
Occupation: Agent, Federal Bureau of Investigation
Military Service: World War One, World War Two

Notes for Charles Batsell Winstead:
F.B.I. Agent who killed John Dillinger.

Letter Written By J. Edgar Hoover to Charles Batsell Winstead on July 23, 1934

Mr. C. B. Winstead,
Division of Investigation,
U. S. Department of
Justice, 1900 Bankers
Building, Chicago, Illinois.

Dear Mr. Winstead:

   I have been advised by Mr. Purvis and Mr. Cowley that it was you who shot and killed John Dillinger. I Wanted to write and to express to you not only my official, but my personal congratulations and commendation for your fearlessness and courageous action in this matter. We are all indeed proud of you. It is particularly gratifying that Dillinger was shot and killed by one of our own men. I am informed that the manner in which you handled yourself on this occasion was indicative if the usual calm, deliberate and at the same time fearless manner which has reflected itself in your work since you entered the Division.
   I wanted you to know that I did personally, as well as officially, appreciate the effort and application which you have given to this case from its inception, and in particular your courageous act of last evening, in shooting and killing this notorious desperado.

                              Sincerely yours,
                              (signed) J. Edgar Hoover
----

9.   **FLORA CLYDE**[3] **SAVAGE** (Charles Edward[2], Edward William[1]) was born on 26 Feb 1896 in Whitewright, Texas. She died on 15 Jan 1987 in Dallas, Texas. She married Claude Augustus Brewer, son of William Eller Brewer and Maude Elizabeth Carson on 13 Jan 1918 in Sherman, Texas. He was born on 24 Sep 1895 in Cumby, Hopkins County, Texas. He died on 30 Dec 1969 in Dallas, Texas.

More About Flora Clyde Savage:
Burial: Restland Memorial Park, Dallas, Dallas County, Texas
Living In: 1920 January 19, 1920 Flora and her daughter, Bette, are living with her mother in Sherman, Grayson County, Texas.
Occupation: 1940 in Dallas, Dallas County, Texas; Public School Teacher

Notes for Flora Clyde Savage:
Texas Death Index gives date of death as January 15, 1987.

Marriahe license was issued January 12, 1918 in Bexar County, Texas. Wedding performed by

F.F. Brown, Pastor of First Baptist Church of Sherman, Texas. Date and place of wedding is not filled out on certificate. Bride's parents were Witnesses. Certificate returned to Frank R. Newton, County Clerk of Bexar County, on January 21, 1918.

More About Claude Augustus Brewer:
Burial: 01 Jan 1970 in Restland Memorial Park, Dallas, Dallas County,
Texas Cause Of Death: Cerebral Hemorhage
Living In: 1930 Dallas, Texas
Occupation: 1917 in Cumby, Hopkins County, Texas; Book Keeper
Occupation: 1920 in Dallas, Dallas County, Texas; Laborer for Telephone
Company
Occupation: 1928 in Dallas, Dallas County, Texas; Salesman for Butler Brothers
Occupation: 1929 in Dallas, Dallas, Texas; Salesman for Butler Brothers
Occupation: 1930 in Dallas, Dallas County, Texas; Mail Order Salesman for Butler Brothers,
Toys
Occupation: 1933 in Dallas, Dallas County, Texas; Salesman for Butler Brothers
Occupation: 1934 in Dallas, Dallas County, Texas; Salesman
Occupation: 1938 in Dallas, Dallas County, Texas; Travelling Salesman
Occupation: 1940 in Dallas, Dallas County, Texas; Factory Representative for Wholesale
Drugs
Military Service: World War One

Notes for Claude Augustus Brewer:

Marriage license was issued January 12, 1918 in Bexar County, Texas. Wedding performed by F.F. Brown, Pastor of First Baptist Church of Sherman, Texas. Date and place of wedding is not filled out on certificate. Bride's parents were Witnesses. Certificate returned to Frank R. Newton, County Clerk of Bexar County, on January 21, 1918.

Claude Augustus Brewer and Flora Clyde Savage had the following children:

21.   i. FLORA ELIZABETH BELLE[4] BREWER was born on 17 Nov 1918 in Texas. She died on 09 Feb 2013 in Tucson, Arizona. She married Carl Henry Ingwer on 08 Jun 1941. He was born on 16 Sep 1917 in Elyria, Ohio. He died on 07 Jun 2000 in Tucson, Arizona.

22.   ii. JAMES ASHLEY BREWER was born on 14 Jun 1922 in Cumby, Hopkins County, Texas. He died on 08 Nov 1989 in Dallas County, Texas. He married Marcelle Yvonne Poteet on 29 Mar 1949. She was born on 30 Nov 1923 in Cooper, Delta County, Texas. She died on 13 Sep 1982 in Texas.

23.   iii. CLAUDE AUGUSTUS BREWER was born on 09 Jul 1930 in Dallas, Dallas County, Texas. He died on 13 Oct 2013. He married Wilda Jean Truitt on 15 Dec 1951. She was born in Jun 1931 in Kansas City, Missouri.

10.   **NINA LEA[3] SAVAGE** (Charles Edward[2], Edward William[1]) was born on 07 May 1900 in Whitewright, Texas. She died on 02 Jul 1982 in Edmond, Oklahoma. She married Al Bryan on 06 Nov 1921 in Sherman, Texas. He was born on 23 Jan 1899 in Texas. He died on 07 Dec 1982 in Edmond, Oklahoma.

More About Al Bryan:
Occupation: 1930 in Okemah, Okfuskee County, Oklahoma; Life Insurance
Agent
Occupation: 1940 in Oklahoma City, Oklahoma; Life Insurance Agent

Al Bryan and Nina Lea Savage had the following children:

  i. WILLIAM JOHN[4] BRYAN was born on 23 Mar 1926 in Oklahoma.

  ii. PAT O. BRYAN was born on 16 May 1931.

11. **WILLIAM PAYNE**[3] **SAVAGE** (Charles Edward[2], Edward William[1]) was born on 23 Sep 1903 in Whitewright, Texas. He died in Jul 1970 in Oklahoma City, Oklahoma. He married Mary Bell Badgett, daughter of Claude Ray Badgett and Annie Bell Bowie on 28 Feb 1925 in Bells, Grayson County, Texas. She was born on 19 Oct 1905 in Bells, Texas. She died on 20 Feb 1964 in Houston, Texas.

More About William Payne Savage:
Burial: 22 Jul 1970 in West Hill Cemetery, Sherman, Grayson County, Texas
Cause Of Death: Heart Attack
Living In: 1935 Amarillo, Texas
Living In: 1940 Living with his sister, Nina Lea and her family, in Oklahoma City, Oklahoma
Occupation: 1926 in Sherman, Grayson County, Texas; Accountant at Hardwicke and Etter Hardware Company
Occupation: 1930 in Amarillo, Texas; Bookkeeper in Wholesale Hardware
Occupation: 1932 in Amarillo, Texas; Clerk for Morrow-Thomas Hardware
Occupation: 1933 in Amarillo, Texas; Clerk for Morrow-Thomas Hardware
Occupation: 1940 in Oklahoma City, Oklahoma; Traveling Salesman for Wholesale Hardware Military Service: U.S. Army, World War 2, (Captain)

Notes for William Payne Savage:
Found dead in his hotel room in Oklahoma City, Oklahoma

More About Mary Bell Badgett:
Burial: 25 Feb 1964 in Quitaque Cemetery, Quitaque, Texas Cause Of Death: Cancer of the Tongue
Living In: 1935 Lubbock, Texas
Occupation: 1940 in Lubbock, Lubbock County, Texas; Stenographer for Life Insurance Company
Occupation: Worked for the Department of State in Washington, D.C.

Notes for Mary Bell Badgett:
Born Mary Bell Badgett. Mary Bell was later changed to Maribel.

William Payne Savage and Mary Bell Badgett had the following children:

24. i. MARIBEL (MARY BELL)[4] SAVAGE was born on 22 Jun 1926 in Sherman, Texas. She died on 14 Feb 2010 in Tampa, Florida. She married Roy Garland Edwards on 08 Apr 1944 in Lubbock, Texas. He was born on 30 May 1922 in Loraine, Texas. He died on 14 Oct 1974 in Tampa, Florida.

25. ii. CLAUDE RAY SAVAGE was born on 02 Jul 1933 in Quitaque, Briscoe County, Texas. He died on 17 Apr 1984 in Tarrant County, Texas. He married Alma Pauline Chitty, daughter of Robert Olos Chitty and Rosalie May Morgan on 09 Dec 1951 in Silverton, Texas. She was born on 01 Aug 1932 in Silverton, Texas.

12. **MARTHA**[3] **MATHIS** (Mary Virginia[2] Savage, Edward William[1] Savage) was born on 18 Jan 1893 in Whitewright, Texas. She died on 22 Sep 1938 in Pahokee, Palm Beach County, Florida. She married **CHARLES DENTON**. He was born on 14 Jan 1895 in Tennessee. He died in Jan 1967 in Palm Beach County, Florida. She married (2) **LUSTER RAY KERR** in 1909. He was born on 21 Jul

1889 in Grayson County, Texas. He died on 23 Nov 1924 in San Angelo, Tom Green
County, Texas.

More About Martha Mathis:
Burial: 24 Sep 1938 in Woodlawn Cemetery, West Palm Beach, Palm Beach County, Florida
Living In: 1920 Martha, as a widow, and her daughter are living with her mother and stepfather in
Justice Precinct 1, Grayson County, Texas.
Occupation: 1920 in Justice Precinct 1, Grayson County, Texas; Office Girl

Notes for Martha Mathis:
Florida death index has date of death as September 22, 1938. Headstone has date of death
as September 23, 1938.

More About Charles Denton:
Occupation: 1928 in Sherman, Grayson County, Texas; Salesman
Occupation: 1930 in South Bay, Palm Beach County, Florida; Truck Farmer
Occupation: 1935 in Palm Beach County, Florida; Rents Filling Station

Charles Denton and Martha Mathis had the following children:

 i. MARY GRACE[4] DENTON was born on 31 Mar 1926 in Grayson County, Texas.

 ii. CHARLES HERMAN DENTON was born on 03 Nov 1928 in Sherman, Grayson County,
Texas. He died on 15 Jun 1953 in San Diego County, California.

  More About Charles Herman Denton:
  Burial: Woodlawn Cemetery, West Palm Beach, Palm Beach County, Florida

More About Luster Ray Kerr:
Occupation: 1910 in Sherman, Grayson County, Texas; Laborer on Dairy Farm
Occupation: 1920 in Justice Precinct 1, Grayson County, Texas; Laborer on Dairy
Farm
Occupation: 1924 in San Angelo, Tom Green County, Texas; Dairyman

Luster Ray Kerr and Martha Mathis had the following child:

 i. MARION BEATRICE[4] KERR was born on 07 Mar 1911 in Sherman, Grayson County,
Texas. She died on 13 May 1994 in Florida. She married (UNKNOWN) BURNS.

  More About Marion Beatrice Kerr:
  Burial: Woodlawn Cemetery, West Palm Beach, Palm Beach County, Florida

13. IRENE FAE[3] SAVAGE (Edward[2], Edward William[1]) was born on 10 Dec 1896 in Whitewright, Texas.
She died on 24 Oct 1976 in Westville, Oklahoma. She married Henry Lightfoot Large, son of
Jonathan A. Large and Sophrona Elizabeth Gossett on 03 Oct 1920 in Texas. He was born on 26
Jun 1895 in Mulberry, Fannin County, Texas. He died on 14 Mar 1963 in Westville, Oklahoma.

More About Irene Fae Savage:
Burial: Westville Cemetery, Westville, Adair County, Oklahoma

More About Henry Lightfoot Large:
Burial: 17 Mar 1963 in Westville Cemetery, Westville, Adair County, Oklahoma

Notes for Henry Lightfoot Large:
Funeral service for Henry L. LARGE, 66, was held Saturday, March 17 at 2 p.m. in the First Baptist church of which he was an active member, with the pastor, Rev. Luther NELSON, officiating. Mrs. Grover HOWARD accompanied Mrs. Paul CARRINGTON, Mrs. Carl ISHMAEL, Mrs. Harold Ray HART, and Fred ALLISON who sang, "Whispering Hope, " "Asleep in Jesus," and "Give Your Heart to the Master."
Mr. LARGE was born June 26, 1895 at Mulberry, Texas, son of Saphrona and Joel C. LARGE and died suddenly Wednesday, March 14, at his home near Westville.
He had been a member of the Baptist church since 1917, having served as Associational Missionary in Grayson County, Texas.
Following his return from World War 1, some of which was spent overseas, he and Miss Irene Fay SAVAGE of Dennison, Texas, were married October 3, 1920. They established their home on the LARGE farm until 1939. To them were born three sons, preceding Mr. LARGE in death. Interment was in Westville Cemetery, under the direction of Roberts Funeral Home.
Active pallbearers were E.L. ANDERSON, J.T. WATSON, D.P. SLEDGE, Gene POTEET, Johnnie ROGERS, W.T. WATSON. Honorary pallbearers were Bill GALBRAITH, Paul CARRINGTON, Carl ISHMAEL, O.B. VEAZEY. Luther WADLEY, Marvin CAGLE, Lee WILLIAMS, Terry WALKER, Jim JONES, Joe WRIGHT, Dee SMITH, Herman WHITELY, Ernest HARMON, Harvey BROWERS, Ferris CABE, Roy GRIFFIN, George HARTMAN, Matt JONES, Frank JOHNDROW, J.S. TOLAND. Flower bearers were Mrs. T.S. PENNINGTON, Mrs. D.W. BUSHYHEAD, Mrs. Herman WHITELY, Mrs. Edith HILLARD, Mrs. Elise NORRIS, Mrs. Nora SINGLETON, Mrs. Ernest HARMON, Mrs. Clara PHILLIPS.
Survivors include his wife, Irene Fay of the home; three daughters, Mrs. Elizabeth JONES of Darby, Colo.; Mrs. Margaret TERRELL, Joplin, Mo.; Mrs. Esther Jane NICHOLS, Hobbs, N.M.; four sons, Harvey and Robert LARGE, Albuquerque, N. Mex.; Dan LARGE, San Antonio, Texas, J.C. LARGE of the home; one sister, Mrs. Alma V. JORDAN, Tempe, Arizona; two nieces and three nephews, Tempe, Ariz.; and several grand nieces and nephews.

Henry Lightfoot Large and Irene Fae Savage had the following children:

      i.   ESTER JANE[4] LARGE.

      ii.   SAMUEL LARGE.

26.   iii. MABEL ELIZABETH LARGE was born on 29 Aug 1922 in Grayson County, Texas. She married Henry Harrison Jones, son of Jessie Albert Jones and Mary Ethel Phillips on 06 Nov 1942 in Muskogee, Oklahoma. He was born on 02 Aug 1919 in Oklahoma. He died on 15 Dec 1985 in Commerce City, Colorado.

      iv. MIRA MARGARET LARGE was born on 26 May 1924 in Texas.

      v.   JOEL CROCKETT LARGE was born on 13 Jan 1926 in Grayson County, Texas.

      vi. HENRY ED LARGE was born on 05 May 1928 in Grayson County, Texas. He died on 22 May 1930 in Denison, Texas.

            More About Henry Ed Large:
            Burial: 23 May 1930 in Oakwood Cemetery, Denison, Texas
            Cause Of Death: Pneumonia

      vii. HARVEY DAVID LARGE was born on 02 Nov 1929 in Denison, Texas. He died on 22 Dec 2003 in New Mexico.

      viii. DANIEL JOSEPH LARGE was born on 24 Dec 1930.

      ix.   SIMON ANDREW LARGE was born on 15 Apr 1932 in Grayson County, Texas.

      x.   ROBERT LEE LARGE was born on 24 Jan 1935 in Grayson County, Texas.

      xi.   SILAS ROY LARGE was born on 18 Jan 1937 in Grayson County, Texas.

14.   HERBERT BURTIS[3] SAVAGE (Edward[2], Edward William[1]) was born on 24 Aug 1900 in Texas. He died on 16 Oct 1960 in Grand Prarie, Dallas County, Texas. He married BESSIE LOU HICKS. She was born on 31 Jan 1901 in Tom Bean, Texas. She died on 05 Feb 1959 in Dallas, Dallas County, Texas.

More About Herbert Burtis Savage:
Burial: 16 Oct 1960 in Restland Memorial Park, Dallas, Texas
Occupation: 1920 in Denison, Grayson County, Texas; Clerk in Retail Grocery Store

Notes for Herbert Burtis Savage:
Death certificate has middle name as "Burt".

More About Bessie Lou Hicks:
Burial: 07 Feb 1959 in Restland Memorial Park, Dallas, Texas

Herbert Burtis Savage and Bessie Lou Hicks had the following child:
      i.   JACK[4] SAVAGE.

15.   VELMA[3] SAVAGE (Edward[2], Edward William[1]) was born on 25 Jan 1902 in Bells, Grayson County, Texas. She died on 18 Apr 1983 in Mesa, Arizona. She married James Thomas Watson, son of Morton Price Watson and Amanda Allethia Goff on 07 Sep 1919 in Denison, Texas. He was born on 11 Oct 1896 in Bells, Grayson County, Texas. He died on 17 Aug 1973 in Mesa, Arizona.

More About Velma Savage:
Burial: Dallas, Texas

More About James Thomas Watson:
Burial: Dallas, Texas

James Thomas Watson and Velma Savage had the following children:

27.   i. EDWARD PRICE[4] WATSON. He married ADA MARIE APPLEBY. She was born on 19 Nov 1921 in Alberta, Canada. She died on 07 Nov 1987 in Redondo Beach, California.

28.   ii.   WILLIAM THOMAS WATSON. He married MILDRED J. BOWERS. He married JOYCE LEMARE.

29.   iii.   CHARLES RICHARD WATSON. He married MARY STONE. He married LEE CRIDER.

30.   iv.   DAVID LYNN WATSON. He married CAROL MARIE KEELE.

      v.   MICHAEL LAVERN WATSON.

      vi.   JAMES ERNEST WATSON was born on 18 Sep 1922 in Bells, Grayson County, Texas. He died on 09 Feb 1962 in Dallas, Texas. He married MARCELLA RIDER.

16.   **LESTER EDWARD[3] SAVAGE** (Edward[2], Edward William[1]) was born on 04 May 1916 in Texas. He died on 22 Sep 1981 in Dallas, Dallas County, Texas. He married **FRANCES LOUISE DEARING**. She died after 22 Sep 1981.

More About Lester Edward Savage:
Burial: 24 Sep 1981 in Grove Hill Memorial Park, Dallas, Dallas County, Texas
Living In: 1940 Living with his mother in Dallas, Dallas County, Texas
Occupation: 1930 in Precinct 2, Grayson County, Texas; Farm Laborer
Occupation: 1940 in Dallas, Dallas County, Texas; Book Keeper in Bakery
Occupation: 1981 ; Industrial Chaplain at Auto Air Conditioning Manufacturer

Lester Edward Savage and Frances Louise Dearing had the following child:

   i.   CAROLYN LOUISE[4] SAVAGE was born on 26 Nov 1944 in Jefferson County, Texas.

Generation 4

17.   **JOSEPH WILLIAM[4] THORN** (Maude Aleene[3] Savage, Charles Edward[2] Savage, Edward William[1] Savage) was born on 09 May 1917 in Sherman, Grayson County, Texas. He died on 29 Oct 1952 in Fort Worth, Tarrant County, Texas. He married Edith Jewell Dick on 10 Sep 1937 in Thackerville, Oklahoma. She was born on 19 Oct 1920 in Denison, Texas.

More About Joseph William Thorn:
Burial: 01 Nov 1952 in West Hill Cemetery, Sherman, Grayson County, Texas
Cause Of Death: Head Injury from Motorcycle Accident
Occupation: Railroad Employee
Military Service: World War Two

Notes for Joseph William Thorn:
Birth date is from birth certificate

Joseph William Thorn and Edith Jewell Dick had the following children:

   i.   BILLY JOE[5] THORN was born on 16 Jul 1938 in Collinsville, Texas. He married CAROLE ANNE SIMPSON. She was born on 15 Nov 1939. He married (UNKNOWN) BROOXIE.

   ii.   RETHEA DARLENE THORN was born on 06 Aug 1939. She married ALFRED BRADSHAW. He was born on 05 Aug 1935.

   iii.   THOMAS ROBERT THORN was born on 25 Oct 1941 in Grayson County, Texas. He married ETHEL STEELE.

   iv.   RICHARD V. THORN was born on 19 Apr 1947. He married DARLEAN (UNKNOWN).

18.   **ALBERT BLEDSOE[4] THORN** (Maude Aleene[3] Savage, Charles Edward[2] Savage, Edward William[1] Savage) was born on 30 Nov 1918 in Dexter, Grayson County, Texas. He died on 27 Jul 2009 in Garland, Texas. He married (1) **HANNELORE HEDWIG MAHLOW** on 29 Mar 1950. She was born on 11 Nov 1923 in Germany. He married (2) **CAROLYN S. MCADAMS** on 20 Sep 1981 in Dallas County, Texas. She was born on 17 Oct 1944.

More About Albert Bledsoe Thorn:
Burial: 05 Aug 2009 in Restland Memorial Park, Dallas, Dallas County, Texas

Occupation: 1940 in Sherman, Grayson County, Texas; Assistant Education Advisor in C.C.C.
Military Service: Bet. 18 Jul 1942-02 Dec 1945 ; U. S. Army, World War Two
Military Service: Bet. 03 Jul 1948-02 Jul 1952; U.S. Army

Notes for Albert Bledsoe Thorn:
Served with the 7th Field Hospital, 3rd Army in Europe during World War Two. Enlisted July 18, 1942 in Dallas, Dallas County, Texas.

Albert Thorn, born Nov. 30, 1918, joined His Savior July 27, 2009 at his home in Garland, TX. He served in WWII with the 7th Field Hospital in the 3rd Army. Campaigns included Normandy, Northern France, the Rhineland, and Central Europe. He received the European-African-M.E. Medal with four Bronze Stars, Good Conduct Medal, Bronze Star Medal, Meritorious Unit Award Medal, and the WWII Victory Medal. He also served in FDR's Civilian Conservation Corps. He is survived by his wife Carolyn, children Charles Thorn and Lorna Wilson. Two grandchildren, several great grandchildren, sister Patricia Jones, three nephews, one niece. Visitation will be Wednesday August 5, 2009 from 10:00 am to 12:00 pm at the funeral home. Committal services with Military Honors will be held at Restland Memorial Park at 12:30 pm August 5, 2009.

Albert Bledsoe Thorn and Hannelore Hedwig Mahlow had the following children:

   31.   i. LORNA LYNETTE^5 THORN was born on 23 Dec 1950. She married Ronald Tucker Wilson on 02 Oct 1976 in Hunt County, Texas.

        ii.   CHARLES RENEE CLARKE THORN was born on 02 Mar 1959 in Travis County, Texas.

19.   **PATRICIA ALTON**^{4} **THORN** (Maude Aleene^3 Savage, Charles Edward^2 Savage, Edward William^1 Savage) was born on 16 Oct 1923 in Dexter, Grayson County, Texas. She died on 18 Aug 2013 in Athens, Henderson County, Texas. She married Kenneth Leroy Jones, son of Howard Lyman Jones and Rebecca Glen Herron on 13 Apr 1946 in Dade County, Florida. He was born on 29 Jul 1920 in Long Branch, New Jersey. He died on 03 Mar 1998 in Sherman, Texas.

More About Patricia Alton Thorn:
Burial: 22 Aug 2013 in West Hill Cemetery, Sherman, Grayson County, Texas

Notes for Patricia Alton Thorn:

SHERMAN - Patricia Thorn Jones, 89, formerly of Sherman, passed away at her home on Sunday, Aug. 18, 2013 in Athens. Graveside services are scheduled for 2 p.m. Thursday, Aug. 22 in West Hill Cemetery. Pastor Leland Samuelson will officiate. Arrangements are under the direction of Dannel Funeral Home.

Mrs. Jones was born Oct. 16, 1923, in western Grayson County, to Joseph Bledsoe Thorn and Maude Aleene Savage Thorn. After graduating from Sherman High School, she went right to work. She was a welder during much of World War II, known to colleagues in the Fort Worth Defense Plant as 'Winnie the Welder.' In 1946, she married Kenneth Leroy Jones in Everglade City, Fla. During Captain Jones' flawless 33-year career as an Eastern Airlines pilot, they made their home in Miami, Fla. While raising her family, Patricia also maintained her Realtor's license and remained an active force in the real estate market. In 1980, the couple 'retired' back to Patricia's home territory. They enjoyed nearly 20 years in Sherman, before Kenneth's death in 1998.

During her retirement years, Patricia was an unparalleled dynamo in numerous organizations. Some of the associations in which she was instrumental are as follows: Dixie Chapter #35 of the United Daughters of the Confederacy; Texas Branch of National Society of Sons and Daughters of the Pilgrims; John Cavet Chapter of the National Society of the United States Daughters of 1812;

Life Member-National Society Daughters of the American Revolution, (Treasurer)-Martha Jefferson Randolph Chapter; Charter Member-Edward Maxey, Sr. Chapter of the National Society Colonial Dames XVII Century (served as President and Organizing Treasurer); Life Member-Order of American Armorial Ancestry; Charter Member-Solomon Bostick Chapter of Daughters of the Republic of Texas (Organizing Registrar and later, President); Charter Member-Nathaniel Pope Chapter of the National Society Daughters of the American Colonists (Organizing Treasurer); Life Member-New England Historic Genealogical Society; Life Member - Presidential Families of America; Life Member of the Order of the Honorable Artillery; Life Member of Order of the Second World War; Perpetual Member of Hereditary Blue Book; Life Member-New England Women, Texas Colony 121; Member of Grayson County Genealogical Society; Life Member-National Society Sons and Daughters of Antebellum Planters 1607-1783; Life Member-Guild of Colonial Artisans and Tradesmen 1607-1783; Member-The Colonial Dames of America; Member-Jamestown Society, Lone Star Chapter; Member-Huguenot Society Founders of Manikin in the Colony of Virginia; Life Member-National Society Descendants of Early Quakers; Member-Grayson County Genealogical Society (Treasurer and Board Member); Member-Houston Genealogical Forum, Connecticut Society of Genealogists, The Rucker Family Society; Life Member-The Walter Palmer Society; Life Member-The Parke Society.

Mrs. Jones is survived by her children, Kenneth Charles Jones (Dian), of Athens, Patricia Quinnelly (Richard), of Bradenton, Fla. and Pamela Wallace (Bill), of Port Orange, Fla.; two nieces, Lorna Wilson and Darlene Bradshaw; and seven grandchildren.

She is preceded in death by her parents; her husband; her daughter, Priscilla Jones; and stepmother, Mary Walker Thorn.

In lieu of flowers, family members encourage memorial donations to Home Hospice of Grayson County, 505 W. Center St., Sherman, TX 75090.

All arrangement s are under the direction of Dannel Funeral Home in Sherman.
Online condolences may be registered at www.dannelfuneralhome.com.

Published in The Herald Democrat on Aug. 21, 2013

More About Kenneth Leroy Jones:
Burial: 06 Apr 1998 in West Hill Cemetery, Sherman, Grayson County,
Texas Occupation: Pilot with Eastern Airlines
Military Service: Bet. 19 Oct 1942-22 Feb 1946; U.S. Army Air Force

Notes for Kenneth Leroy Jones:
Enlisted in U.S. Army Air Force at Camp Blanding, Florida on October 19, 1942. Attained rank of sergeant.

Kenneth Leroy Jones and Patricia Alton Thorn had the following children:

32.   i. PATRICIA MARIE^5 JONES was born on 18 Dec 1946 in Dade County, Florida. She married JAMES DOUGLAS MCDOWALL. He was born on 18 Nov 1946 in Florida. She married RICHARD QUINNELLY.

33.   ii. PAMELA ALEENE JONES was born on 19 Aug 1950 in Miami, Florida. She married WILLIAM OWEN WALLACE. He was born on 22 Jan 1950 in Miami, Florida.

        iii. KENNETH CHARLES JONES was born on 27 Feb 1952 in Miami, Florida. He married DIAN SATTERFIELD. She was born on 14 May 1948.

iv. PRISCILLA ANNETTE JONES was born on 16 Apr 1957 in Miami Shores, Florida. She died on 07 Mar 1961.

20. THOMAS PAYNE[4] THORN (Maude Aleene[3] Savage, Charles Edward[2] Savage, Edward William[1] Savage) was born on 30 Dec 1925 in Delaware Bend, Texas. He died on 28 Sep 1990 in Galveston, Texas. He married NANCY COQUESE MCLANE. She was born on 13 Mar 1926 in Sherman, Texas. She died on 15 Jan 1979 in Harbor City, Los Angeles County, California. He married SANDRA WALSH.

More About Thomas Payne Thorn:
Burial: Oak Wood Cemetery, Whitesboro, Grayson County,
Texas
Military Service: Bet. 18 Sep 1943-22 Feb 1947; U.S. Navy
Military Service: Bet. 29 Jul 1948-30 Jan 1950; U.S. Army
Military Service: Bet. 09 Oct 1950-28 Jul 1954; U.S. Navy

More About Nancy Coquese McLane:
Burial: Green Hills Memorial Park, Rancho Palos Verdes, Los Angeles County, California

Thomas Payne Thorn and Nancy Coquese McLane had the following children:

i. SHERRY LYNN[5] THORN was born on 29 Mar 1948 in Grayson County, Texas.

ii. JOSEPH THOMAS THORN was born on 04 May 1949.

iii. GREGORY BRYAN THORN was born on 16 Nov 1950 in Grayson County, Texas. He married Debra E. Donica on 24 Feb 1970 in Grayson County, Texas. She was born about 1955.

Thomas Payne Thorn and Sandra Walsh had the following child:

iv. MICHAEL DAREN THORN was born on 28 Sep 1966 in Los Angeles, California. He married BELINDA CRAVEN.

21. FLORA ELIZABETH BELLE[4] BREWER (Flora Clyde[3] Savage, Charles Edward[2] Savage, Edward William[1] Savage) was born on 17 Nov 1918 in Texas. She died on 09 Feb 2013 in Tucson, Arizona. She married Carl Henry Ingwer on 08 Jun 1941. He was born on 16 Sep 1917 in Elyria, Ohio. He died on 07 Jun 2000 in Tucson, Arizona.

More About Flora Elizabeth Belle Brewer:
Burial: East Lawn Palms Cemetery & Mortuary, Tucson, Pima County, Arizona
Occupation: 1940 in Dallas, Dallas County, Texas; Assistant Librarian at Private School

Notes for Flora Elizabeth Belle Brewer:
Bette Belle Ingwer 94, passed away peacefully surrounded by her family on February 9, 2013 in Tucson, AZ. She was preceded in death by her loving husband Carl whom she was married to for 60 years, and brother James Ashley Brewer. She was a graduate on Southern Methodist University and a life member of Delta Delta Delta Sorority. A strong supporter of U of A athletics, she was also a member of the Presidents Club of the University of Arizona Foundation. Her other memberships included MO Club, Tucson Country Club, past president of Assistance League of Tucson, DAR, Arizona Sonora Desert Museum, and the Tucson Botanical Gardens. She also belonged to Friends of Western Art, Patio Garden Club, TMC Auxiliary, and was a past member of Desert Club. Her hobbies and passions included traveling the world with her family, golfing, playing bridge and Mah-Jong, reading, and entertaining. She especially enjoyed the Tucson Performing Arts. Bette Belle is survived by daughters, Carla Hamilton of Phoenix, Shirley Burns (Dan Lee) of Las Vegas, and brother Claude A. Brewer of Dallas. Her grandchildren include Dustin Hamilton

(Paige) and Melissa Johnson, both of Phoenix, and David Hoff (Margaret) of Virginia. She leaves three great-granddaughters, Courtney and Allison Hamilton, Mary Hoff and great-grandson, John Hoff. In lieu of flowers the family suggests donations to . At Bette Belle's request there will be no services. Arrangements by EAST LAWN PALMS MORTUARY.

More About Carl Henry Ingwer:
Burial: East Lawn Palms Cemetery & Mortuary, Tucson, Pima County, Arizona
Military Service: 13 Mar 1941 in Cleveland, Ohio; Enlisted in U.S. Army

Carl Henry Ingwer and Flora Elizabeth Belle Brewer had the following children:

     i.   CARLA BELLE[5] INGWER was born on 19 Mar 1943 in San Antonio, Texas. She married BRUCE HAMILTON.

    ii.   SHIRLEY JANE INGWER was born on 12 Jul 1949.

22.   **JAMES ASHLEY**[4] **BREWER** (Flora Clyde[3] Savage, Charles Edward[2] Savage, Edward William[1] Savage) was born on 14 Jun 1922 in Cumby, Hopkins County, Texas. He died on 08 Nov 1989 in Dallas County, Texas. He married Marcelle Yvonne Poteet on 29 Mar 1949. She was born on 30 Nov 1923 in Cooper, Delta County, Texas. She died on 13 Sep 1982 in Texas.

More About Marcelle Yvonne Poteet:
Burial: Oaklawn Cemetery, Cooper, Delta County, Texas

James Ashley Brewer and Marcelle Yvonne Poteet had the following child:

     i.   JAMES ASHLEY[5] BREWER was born on 16 Apr 1950.

23.   **CLAUDE AUGUSTUS**[4] **BREWER** (Flora Clyde[3] Savage, Charles Edward[2] Savage, Edward William[1] Savage) was born on 09 Jul 1930 in Dallas, Dallas County, Texas. He died on 13 Oct 2013. He married Wilda Jean Truitt on 15 Dec 1951. She was born in Jun 1931 in Kansas City, Missouri.

Notes for Claude Augustus Brewer:

BREWER, JR., CLAUDE AUGUSTUS
July 9, 1930 - October 14, 2013

On Monday, October 13, 2013 passed away at 83 surrounded by family. Claude lived a very full life and leaves family and many friends behind. His departure leaves a great void within us all.

Claude served proudly as a 1st Lieutenant in the United States Air Force and was stationed in Germany in 1955. He returned to the United States to begin civilian life and continue to build his life and family with his wife Wilda.

As a strong advocate of sports, Claude felt being part of a team and involved in sports helped to build leadership, discipline, and teamwork. He was deeply involved with the YMCA and the Youth group activities which included his volunteer group as camp counselor for many years at Camp Grady Spruce. He was previously involved in Camp Crockett as youth camper and counselor.

Personally he was always involved with sports which included bowling, softball and of course golf! This is evident with the many trophies you all have seen displayed through his home and spoken about in his many stories. He continued his love of sports through coaching his own children and their friends through numerous little league sports within YMCA and SVAA. When asked he was quick to recount all the stats of each team he was involved in and any other sport stats that would be relevant to the success of his teams.

Claude was also an avid outdoorsman from his youth. He hunted with his close friends regularly. He and friends brought home all they caught for his mother to prepare. His love for hunting was passed along to his children and grandchildren. He thoroughly enjoyed spending time with friends and family while away on their hunting trips.

Claude was an intricate part of East Dallas Christian Church since birth in 1930. His devotion to the church ran deep as he was involved with so many activities. He served many years as a deacon and was a great supporter of the youth group activities within the church as well.

Late in life Claude began his work with the North Dallas High School Alumni Association in 1991. He was a pivotal part of the program which helped develop scholarships and worked to enhance the educational needs of the school. Claude was an important factor in the 2006 and 2012 Anex additions as well as the dedication of the Texas Historical Commission marker that presented in August 24, 2013.

Being a historical buff, his goal was to create a living history of the people who attended NDHS as well as coaching the young people to strive for excellence. Sports academics and achievements were all equally noted by him and he was always there to recognize those achievements. Whatever NDHS expressed a need for, Claude met the challenge.

A celebration of his life and his dedication to his family and friends will be held on October 18, 2013 at 2:30 at the Restland Memorial Chapel with visitation on October 17, 2013 from 6 pm - 8 pm.

Claude is survived by his wife Wilda Brewer, children Cindy Davis and spouse Michael Davis, Susan Galanopoulos and spouse John Galanopoulos, Claude Brewer III and spouse Kelli Brewer, Chuck Brewer and spouse Claudia Brewer, Connie Ohm and spouse Michael Ohm as well as grandchildren Alec Davis, Rhiannon Davis, Nikolaos Galanopoulos, John Galanopoulos, Kathryn Yokum and spouse Anthony Yokum, Brandon Brewer, Chase Brewer, Suzanne Brewer, Trevor Clarke and Madelyn Ohm.

Claude Augustus Brewer and Wilda Jean Truitt had the following children:

    i.   CYNTHIA ANNETTE[5] BREWER was born on 27 Jul 1952.

    ii.   SUSAN JEAN BREWER was born on 30 Jul 1956.

    iii.   CLAUDE AUGUSTUS BREWER was born on 10 Jan 1958.

    iv.   CHARLES ASHLEY BREWER was born on 15 Jan 1960.

    v.   CONSTANCE ALLISON BREWER was born on 18 Sep 1964.

24.   **MARIBEL (MARY BELL)[4] SAVAGE** (William Payne[3], Charles Edward[2], Edward William[1]) was born on 22 Jun 1926 in Sherman, Texas. She died on 14 Feb 2010 in Tampa, Florida. She married Roy Garland Edwards on 08 Apr 1944 in Lubbock, Texas. He was born on 30 May 1922 in Loraine, Texas. He died on 14 Oct 1974 in Tampa, Florida.

More About Maribel Savage:
Burial: 18 Feb 2010 in Pleasant Grove Cemetery, Durant,
Florida
Living In: 1935 With her mother in Lubbock, Texas
Living In: 1940 With her maternal grandparents in Quitaque, Briscoe County, Texas

Notes for Maribel (Mary Bell) Savage:
Born Mary Bell Savage but known as Maribel most of her life. Original birth certificate does not have a first name and amended birth certicate, filed June 20, 1952, has Maribel for her first name.

More About Roy Garland Edwards:
Burial: 17 Oct 1974 in Pleasant Grove Cemetary, Durant, Florida
Military Service: Bet. 1942-1964; U.S. Air Force (Major)

Roy Garland Edwards and Maribel (Mary Bell) Savage had the following children:

34.   i. DAVID GARLAND[5] EDWARDS was born on 21 May 1945 in Fort Sumner, New Mexico. He married Hope Ellen Stewart on 09 Mar 1968 in Tampa, Florida. She was born on 27 Jun 1949 in South Perry, Ohio.

     ii. ROBERT MARION EDWARDS was born on 11 Dec 1946 in Lubbock, Texas. He died on 13 Feb 2010 in San Francisco, California.

         More About Robert Marion Edwards:
         Cause Of Death: Lung Cancer

25.   **CLAUDE RAY[4] SAVAGE** (William Payne[3], Charles Edward[2], Edward William[1]) was born on 02 Jul 1933 in Quitaque, Briscoe County, Texas. He died on 17 Apr 1984 in Tarrant County, Texas. He married Alma Pauline Chitty, daughter of Robert Olos Chitty and Rosalie May Morgan on 09 Dec 1951 in Silverton, Texas. She was born on 01 Aug 1932 in Silverton, Texas.

More About Claude Ray Savage:
Burial: Moore Memorial Gardens, Arlington, Texas
Cause Of Death: Heart Attack
Living In: 1935 With his mother in Lubbock, Texas.
Living In: 1940 With his maternal grandparents in Quitaque, Briscoe County, Texas.
Military Service: ; U. S. Army

Claude Ray Savage and Alma Pauline Chitty had the following children:

35.   i. RICKY RAY[5] SAVAGE was born on 10 Apr 1955 in Fort Huachuca, Arizona. He married Roxanna May Brake on 20 Jun 1975 in Tarrant County, Texas. She was born in 1956.

36.   ii. RANDY LYNN SAVAGE was born on 20 Aug 1959 in Odessa, Ector County, Texas. He married Robin Marie Tackenberg on 25 May 1985 in Arlington, Texas. She was born about 1961.

26.   **MABEL ELIZABETH[4] LARGE** (Irene Fae[3] Savage, Edward[2] Savage, Edward William[1] Savage) was born on 29 Aug 1922 in Grayson County, Texas. She married Henry Harrison Jones, son of Jessie Albert Jones and Mary Ethel Phillips on 06 Nov 1942 in Muskogee, Oklahoma. He was born on 02 Aug 1919 in Oklahoma. He died on 15 Dec 1985 in Commerce City, Colorado.

Henry Harrison Jones and Mabel Elizabeth Large had the following children:

     i. HENRY ALBERT[5] JONES was born on 26 Jan 1947. He died on 13 Dec 2000 in Commerce City, Colorado.

     ii. JACKIE L. JONES. He married WENDY (UNKNOWN).

27.   **EDWARD PRICE[4] WATSON** (Velma[3] Savage, Edward[2] Savage, Edward William[1] Savage, James

Thomas, Morton Price). He married **ADA MARIE APPLEBY**. She was born on 19 Nov 1921 in Alberta, Canada. She died on 07 Nov 1987 in Redondo Beach, California.

More About Ada Marie Appleby:
Burial: 10 Nov 1987 in Green Hills Cemetery, Los Angeles County, California

Edward Price Watson and Ada Marie Appleby had the following children:

37.   i.   MARGARETE JANE[5] WATSON. She married GARY ERWIN WARNER.

        ii.   VELMA LOUISE WATSON. She married TERRILL WILLIAM KORELL.

       iii.   BARBARA JOAN WATSON.

       iv.   RALPH EDWARD WATSON.

28.   **WILLIAM THOMAS[4] WATSON** (Velma[3] Savage, Edward[2] Savage, Edward William[1] Savage, James Thomas, Morton Price). He married **MILDRED J. BOWERS**. He married **JOYCE LEMARE**.

William Thomas Watson and Mildred J. Bowers had the following children:

        i.   RICKY[5] WATSON.

       ii.   RANDY WATSON. She married STEVE BILSING.

William Thomas Watson and Joyce LeMare had the following child:

       iii.   TINA WATSON.

29.   **CHARLES RICHARD[4] WATSON** (Velma[3] Savage, Edward[2] Savage, Edward William[1] Savage, James Thomas, Morton Price). He married **MARY STONE**. He married **LEE CRIDER**.

Charles Richard Watson and Mary Stone had the following children:

        i.   PAUL RICHARD[5] WATSON.

       ii.   BROOK EARL WATSON.

30.   **DAVID LYNN[4] WATSON** (Velma[3] Savage, Edward[2] Savage, Edward William[1] Savage, James Thomas, Morton Price). He married **CAROL MARIE KEELE**.

David Lynn Watson and Carol Marie Keele had the following children:

        i.   CAROL SUE[5] WATSON. She married DAVID STERLING CLINE.

       ii.   DAVID ALAN WATSON. He married PATRICE THOMSEN.

       iii.   DEBRA KAY WATSON. She married KEVIN D. TAYLOR.

       iv.   JIMMIE LYNN WATSON.

       v.   JASON HOWARD WATSON.

Generation 5

31.   **LORNA LYNETTE[5] THORN** (Albert Bledsoe[4], Maude Aleene[3] Savage, Charles Edward[2] Savage, Edward William[1] Savage) was born on 23 Dec 1950. She married Ronald Tucker Wilson on 02 Oct 1976 in Hunt County, Texas.

Ronald Tucker Wilson and Lorna Lynette Thorn had the following child:

    i. WALLIS TUCKER[6] WILSON was born on 21 Apr 1978 in Hunt County, Texas. Wallis Tucker married an unknown spouse on 02 Oct 1976 in Hunt County, Texas.

32. **PATRICIA MARIE**[5] **JONES** (Patricia Alton[4] Thorn, Maude Aleene[3] Savage, Charles Edward[2] Savage, Edward William[1] Savage) was born on 18 Dec 1946 in Dade County, Florida. She married **JAMES DOUGLAS MCDOWALL**. He was born on 18 Nov 1946 in Florida. She married **RICHARD QUINNELLY**.

James Douglas McDowall and Patricia Marie Jones had the following children:

    i. JAMES PATRICK[6] MCDOWALL was born on 16 Mar 1969.

    ii. DANIEL YOUNGLOVE MCDOWALL was born on 23 Apr 1971.

33. **PAMELA ALEENE**[5] **JONES** (Patricia Alton[4] Thorn, Maude Aleene[3] Savage, Charles Edward[2] Savage, Edward William[1] Savage) was born on 19 Aug 1950 in Miami, Florida. She married **WILLIAM OWEN WALLACE**. He was born on 22 Jan 1950 in Miami, Florida.

William Owen Wallace and Pamela Aleene Jones had the following children:

    i. WILLIAM OWEN[6] WALLACE was born on 17 Jun 1972.

    ii. KENNETH ROBERT WALLACE was born on 14 Sep 1974.

    iii. HEATHER ALEENE WALLACE was born on 16 Jul 1976.

    iv. MARY PRISCILLA WALLACE was born on 20 Dec 1978.

    v. THOMAS GLENN WALLACE was born on 01 Mar 1980.

34. **DAVID GARLAND**[5] **EDWARDS** (Maribel (Mary Bell)[4] Savage, William Payne[3] Savage, Charles Edward[2] Savage, Edward William[1] Savage) was born on 21 May 1945 in Fort Sumner, New Mexico. He married Hope Ellen Stewart on 09 Mar 1968 in Tampa, Florida. She was born on 27 Jun 1949 in South Perry, Ohio.

David Garland Edwards and Hope Ellen Stewart had the following children:

38.   i. DIANA GAIL[6] EDWARDS was born on 28 Mar 1969. She married Mark Gregory Simmons on 23 Dec 1988 in Plant City, Florida.

39.   ii. DARLENE MARIE EDWARDS was born on 28 Dec 1970. She married Randall Edward Thompson on 12 Sep 1993 in Pickerington, Ohio.

    iii. PATRICIA ANNE EDWARDS was born on 20 Oct 1972 in October 20, 1972.

35. **RICKY RAY**[5] **SAVAGE** (Claude Ray[4], William Payne[3], Charles Edward[2], Edward William[1]) was born on 10 Apr 1955 in Fort Huachuca, Arizona. He married Roxanna May Brake on 20 Jun 1975 in Tarrant County, Texas. She was born in 1956.

Ricky Ray Savage and Roxanna May Brake had the following children:

    i. MICHELLE LYNN[6] SAVAGE was born on 31 Aug 1982.

    ii. MELISSA SAVAGE was born in 1984.

36. **RANDY LYNN**[5] **SAVAGE** (Claude Ray[4], William Payne[3], Charles Edward[2], Edward William[1]) was born on 20 Aug 1959 in Odessa, Ector County, Texas. He married Robin Marie Tackenberg on 25

May 1985 in Arlington, Texas. She was born about 1961.

Relationship Notes for Randy Lynn Savage and Robin Marie Tackenberg:
Married at Northside Baptist Church, Arlington, Texas.

Randy Lynn Savage and Robin Marie Tackenberg had the following children:
- i.   TAYLOR MARIE[6] SAVAGE was born on 25 Nov 1993 in Tarrant County, Texas.
- ii.   JENNIFER LYNN SAVAGE was born on 15 Mar 1995 in Tarrant County, Texas.

37.   **MARGARETE JANE[5] WATSON** (Edward Price[4], Velma[3] Savage, Edward[2] Savage, Edward William[1] Savage, Edward Price[4], James Thomas, Morton Price). She married **GARY ERWIN WARNER**.
Gary Erwin Warner and Margarete Jane Watson had the following children:
- i.   MATHEW JASON[6] WARNER.
- ii.   DEREK JOHNATHAN WARNER.
- iii.   AMY ELIZABETH WARNER. She married CAMERON CLARE ALDER.
- iv.   KATHERUNE KYUNG WARNER.

Generation 6

38.   **DIANA GAIL[6] EDWARDS** (David Garland[5], Maribel (Mary Bell)[4] Savage, William Payne[3] Savage, Charles Edward[2] Savage, Edward William[1] Savage) was born on 28 Mar 1969. She married Mark Gregory Simmons on 23 Dec 1988 in Plant City, Florida.

Mark Gregory Simmons and Diana Gail Edwards had the following children:
- i.   MARK GREGORY[7] EDWARDS was born on 20 Jun 1988 in Plant City, Florida. He married Julie Ann Mercer on 17 Feb 2007 in Wellston, Ohio. She was born on 28 May 1988.
- ii.   DAVIAN GAIL SIMMONS was born on 12 Feb 1991 in Monroe, North Carolina.

39.   **DARLENE MARIE[6] EDWARDS** (David Garland[5], Maribel (Mary Bell)[4] Savage, William Payne[3] Savage, Charles Edward[2] Savage, Edward William[1] Savage) was born on 28 Dec 1970. She married Randall Edward Thompson on 12 Sep 1993 in Pickerington, Ohio.

Randall Edward Thompson and Darlene Marie Edwards had the following children:
- i.   TREVOR[7] THOMPSON was born on 11 Sep 1995.
- ii.   VICTORIA KATHLEEN THOMPSON was born in May 1997.